Brand Opening

*Using open-source collaboration principles to
create BIG ideas for brands and beyond*

John Palumbo

ISBN-13: 978-1475213133

For my parents who, after all this time, still have no idea what I do for a living

Contents

Foreword

These days, we're all out there waving the "innovation" flag. The problem is, a lot of us are having a tough time delivering on that promise. That's because when the time comes to innovate, we continue relying on creative approaches designed around the flawed methodology that, *"the target audience and core customer know all."*

The goal of this book is to help you break out of that cycle, by introducing you to a unique innovation approach inspired by the open-source movement. At first, it might make you a bit uncomfortable, since it challenges many of the more traditional idea-generation methodologies. But I'm going to do my best to get you comfortable with it and put you in a position to seamlessly weave it into your creative repertoire.

Before we dive into the approach, there are a few things you should know about this book and me.

First, this is much shorter than a traditional business book. In fact, it might make more sense to call it a manifesto, instead of a book (wow, I sound like Jerry Maguire calling his work a *"mission statement, not a memo"*). Either way, I purposely kept it short, because I figured, if you are anything like me, you probably don't have the time to read another 400-page business book. Especially one that overdoes it with examples, case studies and research and has you saying, *"Okay, I get it, move on already."* I'm going to respect your time and intelligence. You'll probably get through this in one sitting and still walk away with a solid amount of knowledge and information.

Second, I want you to know that I'm not a fan of the term "crowdsourcing." It's overused and in many cases being bastardized by companies trying to jump on the bandwagon.

However, I'm sure some of you will want to paint this book with that brush. If you do, keep in mind that crowdsourcing is about the "crowd" you "source" and I will be discussing a much more <u>unique</u> and <u>powerful</u> crowd than the ones you typically hear about.

Lastly, I struggled with whether or not the word "brand" should even be in the title, because the approach I'm going to discuss can be applied well beyond brands. It can be applied across departments and teams. It can be applied across industries. It can even be applied to everyday problems. In the end, I stuck with *Brand Opening*, since that's the name of the process I live-and-breathe every day at my company.

So, dive into it. Tear pages out of it. Bookmark sections of it. Steal from it. Build on it. Tweet great things about it. Post bad things about it. But, most importantly, THINK about it!

6

1

It's Time to Open Up

I spend a good amount of time working with the people responsible for delivering innovation at brands and companies. And if there's one thing I've noticed, it's that many of them place a great deal of importance on understanding (and even including) the "target audience" and "core customer."

Well, I'm going to kick things off with a quote by one of the greatest innovators in history, Henry Ford, which challenges the importance of those sources. He said:

"If I asked my customers what they wanted, they would have said a faster horse."

Obviously, his point was – if you want to create new ideas, you can't solely rely on those conventional and predictable sources for inspiration and stimuli, such as the target audience and the core customer. Yet, when it comes time to innovate, we forget all about Mr. Ford and spring back to relying on those same old sources.

Why do we do it? Because the ridiculous notion that *"the target audience and core customer know all"* has been hammered into our brains for years-and-years. So much so, that even the <u>new</u> creative approaches we decide to try are designed around utilizing input from those sources. We simply can't escape. And we need to, because we're MISSING OUT on a whole universe of untapped creativity and opportunity for our brands and companies.

Good news! I'm going to introduce you to an OPEN-SOURCE methodology that will help you see beyond those same old sources, discard the flawed idea that *"the target audience and core customer know all"* and ensure you stop "missing out."

An Open-Source History Lesson

You have probably heard the term "open-source," but you might be a bit fuzzy about its origin. So, here's a quick, down-and-dirty open-source history lesson by collaboration consultant, James Cherkoff, which sums it up nicely:

Open Source started when <u>programmers</u> began collaborating online to build new technical platforms and systems. Freed from institutional red-tape, hierarchy and shareholder responsibility the ideas flowed fast and furious through these online communities.

At the heart of the process was the community's willingness to share programming 'source code', albeit under certain conditions. And so the Open Source Movement was born. By any measure, the results have been staggering. Linux, a computer operating system, was one of the first big breakthroughs.

Over time, the open-source movement spread to other industries and interests. Cherkoff cites the following examples:

- *The Creative Commons license is a new type of copyright (nicknamed copyleft) created by an Open Source community that gives artists the flexibility to collaborate.*

- *Wikipedia is an Open Source encyclopedia containing 1.3 million articles in eight different languages, all written, developed and maintained by people around the world.*

- *Ohmynews is an Open Source Korean newspaper written by more than 40,000 individual citizens.*

And while these examples are all from very different industries and areas, they still maintain the integrity of the original open-source movement (inspired by those programmers) by allowing input of <u>different</u> agendas, perspectives and approaches to meet a core objective.

Bringing Open-Source to Brands

Since open-source approaches have proven extremely effective in the technology space and beyond, I believe that more <u>brands</u> and <u>companies</u> need to adopt the model and enable the input of many <u>different</u> disciplines, talents, experiences and perspectives to ignite breakthrough ideas and uncover new solutions to formidable problems.

And I'm not alone when it comes to this belief. There's a lot of research available to support the fact that innovative solutions and ideas are more likely to happen when you throw the doors OPEN and collaborate with all different people with all different perspectives. If you'd like to see some of the research, studies and cases, just read some of these:

- *Medici Effect: What Elephants and Epidemics Can Teach Us About Innovation.* By Frans Johansson

- *Why Not?: How to Use Everyday Ingenuity to Solve Problems Big*

And Small. By Barry Nalebuff and Ian Ayres

- *Connect and Develop: Inside Procter & Gamble's New Model for Innovation.* By Larry Huston and Nabil Sakkab (Harvard Business Review)

- *The Open Innovation Revolution: Essentials, Roadblocks, and Leadership Skills.* By Stefan Lindegaard and Guy Kawasaki

- *Crowdsourcing: Why the Power of the Crowd Is Driving the Future of Business.* By Jeff Howe

Since you're probably too busy to tackle the entire reading list above, I'm going to take you through the most significant <u>benefits</u> of collaborating with all different perspectives that I've culled from those resources (and others), as well as my own personal experience working in this space.

The Benefits of Collaborating with Different Perspectives

1. You'll get fresh and unbiased perspectives and ideas: You might not realize it (or want to admit it), but when the time comes to create new ideas for the brand or project you work on every day, your creativity is severely limited.

What happens is this – over time, countless barriers and rules get programmed into your brain, making it impossible for new ideas to form. It's as if there's this idea-destroying terrorist living in your subconscious who sees the germ of a new and exciting idea forming and it immediately starts whispering in your ear all the reasons why you <u>can't</u> do it or why it <u>won't</u> work and ends up killing the idea before it ever has a chance to take shape.

When you throw open the doors and collaborate with individuals across different disciplines, backgrounds and interests, you will find that some of those individuals know <u>nothing</u> about your brand, industry, target audience or objective. That might scare you at first, but you need to remember that oftentimes "ignorance is bliss." In other words, these people aren't aware of the barriers and rules that are hampering your creativity, and their "ignorance" allows them to freely bring fresh, exciting and worthwhile, thinking to the table.

This point was addressed by the president of Chevrolet Europe, Wayne Brannon, in an article about his search for a breakthrough marketing idea:

According to Brannon, marketing can get "tired and a bit vanilla" when those involved are too close to the brand. He added: "I believe that the ideas that you get from people who are not that close to your brand are often a little bit richer."

Since proximity is an archenemy of creativity, collaborating with outside perspectives will provide you with the innovative, new thinking your subconscious has been programmed to squash.

2. You'll bring a new set of creative eyes to your business: Another benefit of throwing open the doors and accessing a collection of diverse individuals, is you will meet <u>creative</u> <u>minds</u> from <u>outside</u> of your industry such as musicians, fashion designers, writers, mobile app developers, chefs, filmmakers, photographers, tattoo artists and more.

These individuals will view your brand, project or objective through their <u>unique</u> creative lens and bring you ideas you would have never imagined.

This excerpt from *The Wall Street Journal* shows that even Nike's CEO, Mark Parker, finds it beneficial to get all different creative perspectives:

For Mr. Parker and other CEOs, the must-see list is growing in number and variety. Nike has long used team sponsorships and star athlete endorsements to market its products and sought advice from athletes for its designs. But he also spends time with musicians, graffiti artists and other <u>creative talent</u>. "I meet regularly with our biggest retail customers but I also go off the beaten path where I can stimulate the right side of my brain and discover new tastes in music, fashion, cuisine," he says.

3. You'll activate a problem-solving machine: Imagine you are sitting in a room with a group of people and everyone is presented with the same problem to solve individually. You might decide to log on to the Internet to find inspiration to solve the issue. Someone else might hold a brainstorm session to solve it. Another person might round up experts to help crack-the-code. While someone else might decide to work through the problem on her own. The point is that each person would use their <u>personal</u> problem-solving techniques to develop solutions.

That's what happens when you access all different minds – they put their tried-and-true approaches to work on behalf of your objective. And you end up with the most powerful problem-solving machine imaginable.

4. You'll meet individuals who possess crucial information: The fourth benefit of opening the doors and collaborating with all different perspectives is that you will meet people who possess insights and information that you will want and need due to the <u>unique</u> <u>connections</u> they have to your brand, category and/or target audience, including:

The Lovers

Your group of diverse individuals is sure to include people who LOVE your brand or company. Obviously, it makes sense to hear their perspective, so you can gauge what's working and leverage it even further.

The Haters

When you tap into all different perspectives you will also come across people who HATE your brand or company. And while you might not think you need to hear what they have to say, you absolutely do, because they will provide you with a list of areas you need to address and improve.

Pizza giant, Dominos, is so committed to improving their offerings, they <u>purposely</u> find people who loathe their product to hear first-hand the issues that need fixing. In fact, they recently ran an ad campaign featuring real people discussing their issues, along with the steps the company has taken to solve them.

The Innovating Users

Whether companies want to admit it or not, there are people who take brands and products and manipulate them to better fit their lives. They may also use those products in ways the company never intended. I like to call them the *Innovating Users*.

If you want to see a perfect example of the Innovating User dynamic, just Google, *"The many uses of Bounce."* You won't believe all the ways people are using Bounce Dryer Sheets. College students put them in their air conditioning vents to make their dorm rooms smell fresher. Women use them to take static out of their hair. Believe it or not, some people even use them as a mosquito repellent.

If you're a member of the Bounce Brand Team hearing these unexpected uses, you might think, *"Hey, that could be a line extension product"* or *"Let's leverage that usage and create a new and unique marketing message to drive volume."*

The Innovating User dynamic is also geographical. Grand Marnier is a Cognac-based, orange-flavored liqueur that most people perceive to be and after-dinner drink served in a classy snifter glass. But, if you head down to Texas and mention Grand Marnier, people will immediately tell you that it is used in the Gold or Cadillac Margarita. If you're working on the Grand Marnier Brand, this "local" usage is something you might want to exploit nationwide. (By the way, if you're a fan of Margaritas, like me, you should ALWAYS ask the bartender to replace the triple sec with Grand Marnier. If you forget to ask and end up with a really lousy Margarita, just order a small shot of Grand Marnier, and pour it in. Trust me!)

If the concept of Innovating Users interests you, I suggest you grab the book *Democratizing Innovation* by MIT professor, Eric Von Hippel. In it, Von Hippel focuses on a variety of examples of consumers tweaking and tinkering with products for the sole purpose of making those products work better for their lives. At one point, Von Hippel hammers home a crucial point that really says it all:

"Innovation by users, provides a very necessary complement to and feedback for manufacturer innovation."

Fortunately, when you collaborate with all different minds, you will encounter some Innovating Users. And they will tell you the unique ways they use and manipulate your brand to fit their lives, so you can leverage those insights.

The Intimates

It seems as if every company I meet with these days tells me their target audience is "moms." If those companies collaborated with all different minds, moms would obviously be represented in that group. However, they would also come across people who are NOT moms, but possess invaluable insights about them, such as:

- The rest of the family. There's no denying that they know moms, right?

- The producers of the TV shows that moms watch. I can guarantee that Steven Levitan is not a mom. However, he is writing and producing the show *Modern Family* that many moms watch. So, he obviously has some insight into what keeps moms entertained.

- The salespeople (who are not moms) at stores like Gap Kids, who interact with moms every day. There's no denying that this group knows a thing or two about moms, especially when it comes to their shopping habits and behavior.

- The male disc jockeys on the radio stations that moms listen to when they're stuck in the car playing the role of chauffer for the kids. If they don't have a perspective on how to keep moms involved and engaged, then no one does.

While these people may not be moms, they know what moms like. They know what moms don't like. They know what motivates moms. They know how to successfully communicate with moms. So, if your target audience happens to be moms, you <u>want</u> and <u>need</u> their perspectives.

My point is, when you collaborate with all different perspectives, you are going to meet people who are <u>not</u> in your target audience, but have an <u>intimate</u> understanding of the segment. They deserve to have their voices heard and you should be listening carefully to everything they have to say.

5. You'll find existing techniques you can use; Intersections: The final benefit of throwing open the doors and collaborating with all different perspectives, is that you'll come across approaches and techniques that individuals already use in their industry, their culture or their everyday lives that can be directly applied as a solution to your objective.

Basically, you're going to uncover "Intersections." If you aren't familiar with this term I recommend you read the book, *The Medici Effect* where author, Frans Johansson, defines The Intersection as:

> *"The place where different disciplines, cultures and backgrounds connect to form new*

ideas and solutions for long-standing problems."

The best way to explain this concept is to tell you about my favorite Intersection example. It comes from beyond the brand world and focuses on a hospital in London called the *Great Ormond Street Hospital Charity.*

According to a story that ran in *The Wall Street Journal*, doctors at the hospital noticed that the staff was struggling with patient "hand-offs," which is essentially when patients are moved from one area of the hospital to another. For example, a patient coming out of surgery would be "handed-off" to the intensive care unit.

It turns out that in all the confusion and chaos of the hospital setting, communication between these different areas was breaking down and it was leading to critical errors. In some cases, medical charts were being mixed up. In other cases, the wrong medical equipment was ending up in patients' rooms.

Knowing they had this issue, the doctors decided to film their (flawed) process and bring the video to individuals who they felt executed hand-offs in high-pressure situations better than anyone else – the Ferrari Formula One Racing Team PIT CREW!

As the pit crew watched the video, they were shocked to see how clumsy and inefficient the hospital's hand-off process was. They observed that no one was leading the process, which would never happen in the pit where the "lollipop man" is the leader. They also noticed how the noise in the hospital was hindering the hand-offs. This was a scenario they could empathize with, since noise is also an issue down on the racetrack. That's why pit crews predominantly operate in silence using a series of non-verbal cues.

Ultimately, the pit crew applied some of their proven techniques to the hospital setting and the hand-off process was reinvented. Most importantly, the errors the hospital was experiencing were drastically reduced.

Come on, who would ever imagine a hospital enlisting a Formula One pit crew for help? But it makes complete sense when you consider that both of them connect (intersect) at the point of executing "hand-offs in high-pressure situations."

You should know that there are different names being used in the innovation space for this concept. While Frans Johansson calls it "The Intersection," others use terms such as, "Lateral Wisdom," "Parallels" or "Adjacencies."

Obviously, the term is irrelevant. What really matters is the fact that when you access diverse perspectives, you will find techniques already being used by unexpected people that can be applied to your business. (A little later, I will take you through a <u>brand-specific</u> Intersection, where a tool used in the car restoration field inspired an idea for a cosmetics company. Who would ever imagine those two industries finding common ground?)

2

Inviting Collaborators to the Open Party

Now that you understand WHY it makes sense to enlist different perspectives for innovation initiatives, it's time to show you HOW to <u>find</u> and <u>recruit</u> a team of diverse collaborators. And the best way for me to do that is by introducing you to my company and showing you how we bring collaborators into the fold.

Introducing BigHeads

Being a true believer in the methodology that *BIG ideas are more likely to happen when you step outside of what you know and collaborate with all different people with different perspectives*, I wanted to make open-source collaboration completely turnkey for businesses that might not have the time, resources or expertise to do it themselves. So, in 2006, I created BigHeads Network.

In a nutshell, BigHeads is a <u>brain trust</u> made up of creative minds, experts, visionaries and problem-solvers from all <u>different</u> backgrounds and talents.

In other words, people like this:

- Furniture Designer
- Mixologist
- University Coach
- Custom Jeweler
- Yoga Instructor
- Cardiologist
- Sports Artist
- Marriage Counselor
- Makeup Artist
- Reality TV Producer
- Mommy Blogger
- Interior Designer
- Photographer
- Gold Medal Winner
- Singer/Songwriter
- Theme-Park Developer
- Sirius Satellite Radio DJ
- Comedian
- Fashion Designer
- Boutique Hotel Developer
- Fiction Writer
- News Anchor
- Magician
- Matchmaker

- Nightlife Doorman
- Celebrity Chef
- Music Teacher
- Tattoo Artist
- Ivy League Professor
- Sustainability Expert
- Fortune 500 CEO
- Philanthropist
- Gentlemen's Club Dancer
- MLB Umpire
- Professional Skateboarder
- Restaurateur
- Navy Seal
- Beekeeper
- App Developer
- Marine Biologist

...and many more.

Since these people are BIG thinkers with BIG ideas, I named them "BigHeads" and I bring them together with companies to uncover unique inspiration, insights, creativity, unexpected connections and Intersections.

Curated Collaboration

Even though our list of BigHeads is much longer than the one I presented above, it seems there is always someone who wants to turn things into a "numbers" game by saying something like, *"We don't need your network. We are BRAND X and we have access to hundreds of thousands of people who 'like' us on Facebook, 'follow' us on Twitter, blagh, blagh, blagh."*

Admittedly, some brands and companies have access to networks of people (via Facebook, Twitter, etc.) that far outnumber ours. However, when it comes to collaboration, numbers mean nothing, because *collaboration is about quality, not quantity.*

Consider this – the more people you collaborate with, the more feedback you will receive. So, if you decide to collaborate with hundreds of thousands of people from your Facebook or Twitter initiatives, you're going to receive hundreds of thousands of responses. And while that might sound great, here's the reality – most of those responses will be useless, because you didn't take the time to make sure those participants could actually provide QUALITY feedback. That means you will have completely wasted valuable time and resources rifling through tons of information that turned out to be…well, garbage!

Look, you don't have to be a rocket scientist to know that wasting resources is not an option for most companies. They want <u>quality</u> <u>thinking</u> and they usually need it <u>quickly</u>. That's why I am a true believer in **Curated Collaboration**, which simply means taking the time to carefully and methodically <u>select</u> and <u>vet</u> potential collaborators.

Yeah, yeah, yeah…I know! You're thinking, *"If you're <u>selecting</u> the BigHeads, then it's not a fully OPEN process."* And you're right. But even though I may not throw the door completely open and invite in everyone, I open it enough to let in individuals who increase the probability of getting me what I want (quality thinking) in the timeframe I need it (quickly).

Curating Your Collaborators

As a big proponent of taking a Curated Collaboration approach, I have developed some strategies for my company to follow as we continue building our team of collaborators. I recommend you consider them as well, when the time comes to build yours.

1. **Search for talent, not degrees**: As we speak, there are lots of people using the term "Intellectual Diversity" to describe the collaborators you should consider for open-source initiatives. I find that term a bit deceiving, because the word "intellectual" immediately makes you think your diverse team needs to be made up of people with advanced education degrees.

Personally, I prefer to use the word TALENT, because people can possess talent and not necessarily have fancy degrees hanging on their wall.

That said, when you're searching for talent, I recommend you bring on board the following types of people, to ensure you end up with the diversity in perspectives needed to innovate:

- Bring on people from all different disciplines

- Bring on people with interesting hobbies or interests (from roller derby skaters to coin collectors)

- Bring on people who have a creative bent (from writers to tattoo artists)

- Bring on people who are proven problem-solvers (from super moms to air traffic controllers)

- Bring on people from different geographies and different cultures

- Bring on people from all different age groups (from seniors who will provide historical perspectives, right down to Millennials who have recently been dubbed, "Generation Innovation")

- Bring on people who have risen to the top of their field

- Bring on people who are entrepreneurial and always challenge the status quo

- Bring on people who you find interesting, even if you can't pinpoint exactly why

2. **Become a talent scout**: You've heard all the stories about celebrities getting "discovered" by some talent scout at the beach or at a baseball game or wherever. Obviously, these scouts realize that talent is everywhere and they keep their eyes open. You should too!

   I might be in a bar and notice the bartender mixing-up some interesting drink concoctions and think, *"He would make a great BigHead."* Or I could be walking through a street fair and meet an incredibly talented artist selling her pieces and invite her to be a BigHead. This past holiday season, I was driving by a house in New Jersey that was so elaborately decorated, I parked my car and joined all the people admiring the house. I asked around a bit and finally met the husband and wife, who were the creative minds responsible for the display. It probably goes without saying that they are now BigHeads.

You should also bring your talent search to the Internet. It amazes me how limiting people are when it comes to their social networks, especially their "professional" networks. They go on sites like LinkedIn and Twitter and only "connect" with or "follow" people from <u>within</u> their industry, category or area of expertise. You need to go <u>beyond</u> those people and start connecting with talent from completely different disciplines and interests. Once you've made these diverse connections, you can consider inviting them to take part in your collaboration initiatives.

3. **Never stop searching**: Your search for talent should be relentless. It should never stop. This is important for a few reasons. First, as you execute your collaboration projects, you will find that some people you've recruited aren't living up to the expectations you initially had for them and they need to be replaced.

Second, if you're bringing on the right talent, you will be dealing with people who have busy schedules and won't have the time to participate in every one of your projects. An ongoing recruiting effort will ensure your initiatives always include a healthy sample of diverse perspectives.

Lastly, you always want to add "new blood" into the mix to keep things interesting.

4. **Create an application:** It's also important for you to institute an application process, preferably online. This will allow you to extend your search beyond people you meet in person, which is absolutely necessary since you need to include talent from all different

geographies. Putting this measure in place will also help you vet potential collaborators.

My company has an online application that anyone from around the world can fill-out to potentially become a BigHead. Applicants answer a series of questions. Some are designed to capture basic personal information. But the more important ones probe further to find out about their experiences, interests and personal and professional accomplishments, so we can make an informed decision as to whether or not they are BigHeads material.

5. **Tap talent to get talent**: Interesting people often associate with other interesting

people. So, leverage the relationships you have with your collaborators to bring on board even more.

At BigHeads, we've been introduced to many of our members by existing members. When I first started the company, these introductions were completely organic and informal. A BigHead would send me an email with the contact information of a friend who they felt should be a member. These days, our members can send our application to people who they think would make great BigHeads and they receive incentives if the people they nominate are accepted.

6. **Have a compelling pitch**: Before you start inviting people to participate in collaboration initiatives, you need to get your "story" straight. In other words, you need to be able to convey who you are, what you're doing, why you want them to get involved and, even, what's in it for them if they decide to participate.

At BigHeads, we created business card "invites" that we distribute to people who we think would make great members. The invite includes a short description of the company along with a PIN code for them to use when signing up. Once they go to our website and enter the code, they get a full description of what BigHeads is all about –

from our overall company philosophy to the incentive structure we have in place to the non-compete agreement they need to execute.

7. **Use your clout**: For those of you reading this who hail from well-known brands and companies, be sure to use that to your advantage when you are recruiting. You might not think working for your company is all that exciting (because you go there every day), but people from outside of your world think it's special. Remember, these people use brands, but they rarely get the chance to MEET the people behind them. And having you invite them to help out, well, that's the icing on the cake. So,

be sure to mention your company name in your initial pitch or introduction.

You Just Created Your Very Own Renaissance

In the 15th century a member of a wealthy Italian banking family, Lorenzo de' Medici, persuaded the top talent of the time to come to Florence, Italy. This included cultural leaders such as philosophers, scientists, financiers, mathematicians, as well as the top artists, including Leonardo da Vinci, and Michelangelo. Historians have surmised that those minds shared ideas and techniques across their different disciplines and that collision of diverse thinking is what sparked the most creative era in history, the Renaissance.

Once you've curated your team of collaborators, you'll have essentially done the same thing as de' Medici and aggregated a pool of unique talent. Collaborating with them will provide you with the diverse perspectives you need to drive creativity.

You could even say that you'll have your very own, modern-day Renaissance on your hands!

3

Let the Brand Opening Begin!

Once you find and recruit your team of diverse collaborators, you'll be ready to execute open-source initiatives. Of course, it probably won't surprise to hear that there are countless ways for you to collaborate with your diverse team. So, once again, I am going to speak from personal experience and take you through my company's step-by-step process, so you have a first-hand account of a proven and road-tested collaboration approach.

Steps to Opening Brands

Before I get started, let me just say that I'm not ramming this process down your throat. You should feel free to follow our steps to the letter, employ the ones you like best, build-on them or just use them for inspiration when developing your own.

Step One: The Download

Not surprisingly, the first thing we do is meet with a company to understand exactly what they need; what's "keeping them up at night." They could be looking for anything from new product ideas to compelling insights to unique distribution opportunities.

Whatever the case may be, this is the step when we receive a comprehensive download about their objective along with any additional information they feel we should have.

Step Two: Building the Project

Once we understand their objective, we develop the project that we distribute to our brain trust of BigHeads. Every project includes the following:

- An <u>overview</u> describing the company's situation and goal. The amount of detail we include in the overview is determined on a case-by-case basis. Sometimes we want the BigHeads to have a lot of information. Other times we purposely keep things vague, which you'll see in an upcoming example.

- <u>Incentives</u> and <u>challenges</u> to boost excitement and participation. While we have our own incentive system for our members, we also encourage companies to provide participants with an incentive gift as a "thank you" for their efforts. We also regularly include <u>optional</u> challenges where winners receive substantial "prizes."

- A series of five-to-eight strategically crafted <u>questions</u>.

Hold on! Let me repeat that last one. *A series of five-to-eight strategically crafted questions.* I stress that, because the questions we develop are truly the lynchpin for every project we execute. If they're not crafted correctly, the project will be in jeopardy.

That said, when developing the questions, we must first surround the company's objective in a way that will <u>involve</u> and <u>interest</u> our BigHeads. We cannot simply use the formal (internal) objective provided by the company back in Step One, because that type of "industry speak" will not resonate with diverse individuals unfamiliar with that vernacular. Our questions need to be all-inclusive and have the ability to engage and interest all of our members, while surrounding the essence of the formal project objective. It's a tall order, but one that needs to be met every time.

Our questions also need to <u>probe</u> for information that our internal team can use as stimuli to develop the <u>final</u> ideas and solutions. Earlier I discussed all the benefits of collaborating with diverse perspectives. Well, this is where those benefits are realized, as our questions are designed to explore the following:

- Our BigHeads personal stories and experiences, in the context of the overall project. This provides us with invaluable anecdotes that spark ideas and/or connections for us to explore and consider.

- Their creative ideas and potential solutions, related to the project. This ensures we get fresh ideas and leverage their unique creative talents and problem-solving techniques.

- Any connections our BigHeads may have to the brand, category and/or target audience. Here we uncover the insights and <u>intimate</u> knowledge they possess, which we can potentially use.

- The techniques and tools they use across their disciplines and cultures, in the context of the project. This is where we identify existing approaches that can potentially be applied to the objective (Intersections).

Probing our brain trust using this line of questioning arms us with such unique <u>ammunition</u>, we are in the perfect position to develop truly innovative solutions.

Speaking of "ammunition," one of the most common mistakes made by brands, companies and agencies that execute collaboration or crowdsourcing initiatives is that they tend to <u>only</u> ask participants for the <u>answer</u> or <u>solution</u>. They forget that it's just as important to ask questions that will uncover <u>ammunition</u> (the stimuli and inspiration they need to create potential solutions).

<u>Step Three: Let 'em Have It!</u>

We then place the project into an <u>online</u> platform and invite the BigHeads to participate. Then, over the next week to ten days, they provide their thoughts, ideas and perspectives.

I should mention that the BigHeads are working ALONE at this point. This step is <u>not</u> about sharing thoughts and ideas. Earlier we discussed the benefit of having people apply their own problem-solving techniques to an issue. This allows them to do just that. If we executed this step as a group workshop or on an online platform where they worked together, their personal problem-solving techniques could potentially be compromised.

Step Four: Connecting-the-Dots

I always like to say that this is the step where the magic happens, because this is when my team and I <u>connect-the-dots</u> between the information (ammunition) we received via the responses and the overall objective. Oftentimes, the connections we make are so unexpected, the companies we work with are left wondering how we were able to even see/make them in the first place.

And while it may seem like magic, it's actually a brain-numbing process that begins with reading each-and-every response to identify the opportunities we feel have the most potential to inspire real and executable solutions. For example, we might notice common themes emerging across responses, which could inspire a key insight the company could exploit. We might read about a personal experience one BigHead has had and set that story aside, because it contains inspiration for an idea. We might learn about a technique being used by someone in his or her industry that we feel could potentially be applied as a solution (an Intersection).

Once we've identified all the areas with the most potential to inspire solutions, we start digging deeper into each one. For example, we would meet with that BigHead and see the technique from his or her industry in action to determine if it could realistically be applied. Some opportunities won't live up to our initial expectations and we will dismiss them altogether. Others will end up acting as the inspiration for our final recommendations.

Step Five: The Open Book

We then deliver a report that we call the "Open Book," which is organized to include a summary of the BigHeads who participated, their unedited responses and a catalog of content that meets the formal project objective.

Step Six: Selection & Refinement

At this point, we've presented our ideas and solutions to the company and they might decide to simply say, *"Thank you"* and utilize their existing processes to <u>select</u> and/or <u>refine</u> their favorite concepts and ideas.

On the other hand, they might want us to remain involved and handle this part of the project. If we do stay involved, our process becomes much more customized, as we execute selection and refinement approaches that make the most sense for the specific project and the company we are working with. For example:

- We sometimes place the ideas from the Open Book into a secure online collaboration platform where hand-picked participants can then work <u>together</u> to select, rate, build and/or further shape them.

- We sometimes host live workshops with select participants to select, rate, build and/or shape the ideas.

- We sometimes format the concepts to fit the evaluation methodology the company traditionally uses, which could range from consumer screenings to focus groups to an internal testing approach.

Basically, we turn our <u>output</u> <u>into</u> <u>input</u> for their go-to concept evaluation approach.

Brand Opening in Action

Now that you've read through each of the steps we take, it's probably a good idea to bring them to life for you by walking you through an actual project that my company executed.

We were asked by a color cosmetics company to help them find new and unique ways to improve the color choosing experience at retail for their core consumer – women. It happens to be very difficult for women to choose the right color when purchasing cosmetics off-the-shelf at mass retailers like Target or CVS. They buy the product thinking the color is perfect and then get it home and realize the color/shade is off. It's even more of an issue when it comes to foundation products, because they must blend perfectly with their skin color.

As you might imagine, more traditional idea-generation companies would attack this project by holding brainstorms or doing research with <u>women</u> <u>only</u>, since they are the company's target consumer. Of course, you now know that would be a BIG mistake. Only engaging the target audience would lead you to <u>miss-out</u> on a host of unique inspiration and stimuli.

My company attacked this challenge by executing our Brand

Opening process, where we access our brain trust made up of women <u>and</u> men from all different disciplines, geographies, talents and interests (the BigHeads). This put us in the position to uncover the diverse perspectives, unexpected connections and Intersections that we needed to develop innovative ideas that met the objective.

At this point, we needed to create a project that ALL our diverse BigHeads could relate to. We couldn't simply go out and ask our members direct questions about *"improving the color choosing experience at retail"* for the cosmetics industry, because that's not their world. That's too self-serving and would most likely lead them to lose interest (maybe even put them to sleep). Instead, we took a step back and focused the project on the broader topic of *"making color choices."* Now THAT is a topic they could all connect with. That's a topic they would all be interested in. That's a topic all of them could address.

With that more relevant focus, we began crafting the questions to ask the BigHeads that would effectively probe their disciplines, experiences and interests to learn about what they do, the things they know, the tools they use and experiences they've had, all in the context of making color choices. To ensure we didn't "lead the witness" and influence their responses, we decided not to mention that this was for a cosmetics company. Here are some examples of the types of questions we posed:

- We probed their personal experiences and asked them to tell us about those times when they purchased something (anything) they were positive was the right color, but it turned out to be wrong. We then probed further to find out what went wrong and how they ended up fixing the issue. As you can imagine, this question alone armed us with loads of inspiration.

- We tapped their creativity and problem-solving skills and asked them to tell us how they would have avoided the issue they encountered in the previous question if money and access were no object. This is the ol' *"What would Bill Gates do?"* innovation question that generates all types of "pie-in-the-sky" thoughts that can be used to inspire executable ideas. (Remember, <u>unrealistic</u> stimuli can oftentimes inspire <u>realistic</u> solutions.)

- We asked them to describe some of the color choosing experiences they had that were seamless and easy. This armed us with all types of proven and effective approaches that could be tweaked to fit the objective.

There were seven questions in total and as we read all of the responses we began uncovering themes, tactics, approaches and tools we could use as stimuli to create ideas against the objective.

In some cases, the BigHeads told us about situations when they purchased something that they thought was the right color and it turned out to be wrong – from clothing items that didn't look the same when they got them home to cars that looked a lot different once they got them off the dealer's lot. Hearing how some of these issues were resolved or handled in future situations armed us with the diverse inspiration we needed.

For example, some BigHeads provided stories about purchasing paint that, once on their walls, looked a lot different than the sample they saw in the store or in the color sample book. In other words, we learned the paint industry faces the exact same problem as cosmetics. People buy it thinking it is the perfect color, but they get it home and find out it's completely wrong.

This led us to do some digging to learn about ways the paint industry is trying to manage the issue. In doing so, we discovered that "light boxes" are installed in many retailers like Lowe's and Home Depot, which allow consumers to see the paint color in all different lighting scenarios (lighting is one of the key factors that leads us to choose the "wrong" color). That led us to consider a light box concept for the cosmetics aisles.

We also heard some simple and straightforward solutions the BigHeads have used to solve the color-choosing problem. One participant even talked specifically about cosmetics (without knowing this project was for a cosmetics company) and explained how she sometimes gets the color wrong, but she is often so close to getting it right, all she needs to do is "shift" to the next (darker or lighter) shade in the sequence. This solution led us to consider ways to incorporate her "shift" behavior into the actual product, by either packaging the sequence of colors together or by introducing a simple way for women to create and/or mix the shift themselves.

We even heard from a car restoration BigHead who told us about a scanning device he uses to mix paint to perfectly match the original color of the cars he restores. We ended up getting on a plane and heading to his shop in South Florida to see the device first-hand and consider if the technology could be applied as a solution. Our thought was, women could "scan" their skin using a branded mobile app on their smart phone and get the perfect foundation product recommendation from the company. I can tell you that the cosmetics company never imagined a potential solution being inspired by the car restoration industry.

Our final report (the Open Book) included a wide range of content, including product ideas, display concepts, digital executions and packaging innovations.

After presenting the report, we worked together with the company to determine which ideas had the most potential to pursue further. In some cases, we needed a bit more information, so we visited or invited in experts who could help. For example, we met with the developers of the scanning tool, that our car restoration BigHead had shown us, to discuss how we could realistically apply that technology to smart phones to develop our "skin scanning" concept.

When the top ideas were identified, we executed one last step. We posted the concepts on a secure online collaboration platform where select members of the company's internal teams worked together (virtually) to shape the concepts and make them market-ready.

I'm sure you'd love to know some of the final ideas. Unfortunately, I am not at liberty to share them. (Hey, I'm happy I got the green light to share as much as I did!) Who cares about the final ideas anyway? The important thing for you to know is that the process provided the cosmetics company with inspiration and ideas that led to innovations that reside in the marketplace (and some that are on their way). And, that never would have happened if they hadn't accessed a brain trust made up of all different perspectives.

Open Opportunities are Endless

The cosmetics case study is obviously just one example, for

one company, focusing on one specific objective. My company has applied the Brand Opening process to meet all different needs. We've developed new products for innovation teams, conceived new distribution opportunities for senior leadership teams, invented signature offerings for start-up ventures, uncovered and exploited untapped market space for research groups, created stand-out marketing campaigns for brand teams and more.

And while those are very brand-centric objectives, this isn't an approach that's exclusive to brands. Collaborating with diverse perspectives can be used in just about <u>any</u> situation where new ideas are necessary or there's a problem that needs solving. The human resources department can use it to tackle recruiting issues. The finance department can use it to develop new revenue models. The high-school football coach can use it to find clever new ways to enlist boosters.

The steps I discussed earlier would need to be tweaked a bit to meet these unique objectives, but the applications for the overall methodology itself are endless. (In fact, as I write this, we are launching a "beyond the brand" offering where we'll be bringing the power and perspectives of our diverse brain trust to social causes and issues. Stay tuned!)

4

Open-Source Collaboration Reminders

There you have it – a comprehensive look at the ins-and-outs of open-source collaboration. I figured it would make sense to leave you with a list of the thirteen (my lucky number) most important things to keep in mind if you decide to take the "open road." Basically, these are the pages you'll want to bookmark or copy or print or tear out so you always have them in front of you.

1. **Remember, quantity does NOT always mean quality:** Now that you've seen the power of collaborating with diverse perspectives, you might be tempted to invite tons of people (all those people who "like" you on Facebook or all those people who "follow" you on Twitter, etc.) to participate in your idea-generation initiatives. Just remember, quantity doesn't mean quality. If you decide to throw the doors wide open, and invite everybody to participate, just make sure you have the resources and patience to comb through a lot of bad ideas to find the great ones.

On the other hand, you could do what my company does and use a "Curated Collaboration" approach, where you hand-pick your collaborators to ensure they are creative minds, experts and problem-solvers who you know will deliver quality thinking...quickly.

2. **Humanize the objective:** When you collaborate with individuals from different backgrounds and disciplines, you need to steer clear of using your internal/industry jargon. Instead, take the time to step back and talk about your objective in more "human" (relevant) terms to ensure they will be interested and want to get involved and participate.

In the cosmetics example I presented, my company did not go out to our BigHeads with the internal company objective of *"improving the color choosing experience at retail."* Instead, we asked them more relevant questions about *"making color choices."*

3. **Get ammunition, not the answer:** The problem with many collaboration and crowdsourcing initiatives (even more traditional brainstorms) is the people facilitating them want and expect the <u>answer</u>. That not only puts unnecessary pressure on participants (not everyone can be creative, because they're being told to be), but it also severely limits the output of the session.

Remember, it's just as important (actually, more important) to design projects to uncover <u>ammunition</u> (stimuli and inspiration). So, instead of asking for the answer or idea, you're better off probing your collaborators' disciplines, experiences, passions and interests to learn about what they do, things they know, tools they use, experiences they've had, all in the context of the issue or the problem you are trying to solve.

4. **Learn to connect-the-dots:** Once you've probed the disciplines, experiences and interests of your diverse collaborators, it's time to begin making connections between the disparate information

you've received and your overall objective.

For example, when my car restoration BigHead started talking about the scanning device he uses to match paint to the original color of the car being restored, I connected-the-dots and said, *"I can apply that technology to mobile phones for women buying cosmetics!"*

Making these types of connections has become second nature for me. But that's because I've been doing this for a long time. If they don't come as naturally to you, start practicing! Constantly remind yourself to make connections between what you're hearing and the project objective. The more you do it, the more automatic it will become.

5. **Remember, collaboration does NOT mean everyone has to work together:** When you talk about collaborating with all different perspectives, people immediately <u>assume</u> those individuals should be working together to build ideas and solve problems. However, some collaboration approaches incorporate a "blind" or "solo" layer where participants work on the problem alone without anyone influencing their thinking or compromising their tried-and-true problem-solving techniques and strategies.

At BigHeads, we often execute the following two-phased

approach to maximize our collaboration opportunities:

<u>Phase I – Blind/Solo Format</u>: We let the BigHeads go at it <u>alone</u> so they can use the problem-solving techniques they're most comfortable with and they give us responses that have not been influenced by others.

<u>Phase II - Team Format</u>: We take the top ideas and thoughts from Phase I and use team-based approaches (from online collaboration platforms to live workshops) where participants can re-focus and begin building on the top ideas <u>together</u>.

Collaboration means something different to everyone. Let your process dictate what it means to you and your organization.

6. **Be flexible and patient:** After you read this book and do research into the concept of collaborating with diverse minds, you're going to find that there are many different ways to do it. Obviously, my company's Brand Opening process is just one approach.

If you decide to give it a shot, just remember there is no "one size fits all" process. You have to find what works for you and your company. Maybe you'll create your own approach. Maybe you'll combine different approaches. Whatever you do, you are going to need to be flexible and patient, because finding the approach you are comfortable with will take time. Here's an excerpt from a *Harvard Business Review* article about P&G's "Connect and Develop" innovation process that brings-to-life my point:

> *P&G's development and implementation of "Connect and Develop" has unfolded over many years. There have been some hiccups along the way, but largely it has been a methodical process of learning by doing, abandoning what doesn't work and expanding what does.*

7. **Do not let confidentiality be a deal breaker:** Understandably,

confidentiality is one of the top concerns many companies have when they first consider executing an open-source collaboration initiative, especially when they are interested in generating early-stage, proprietary ideas.

Fortunately, there are always steps you can take to ensure your project remains protected. For example, at my company we put the following systems in place to make certain our projects are 100% secure:

- All of our members execute a non-compete agreement.

- We never use industry jargon when reaching out to our BigHeads, because they would most likely lose interest in the project. Instead, we recreate the objective to make it more relevant for our members. This can also serve to conceal the formal (and, often, confidential) objective, from the participants.

- Even though a brand's stature can help boost participation, it is also possible to design projects where the brand/company is not revealed. In the cosmetics case study discussed earlier, the BigHeads did not know the company sponsoring the project (come to think of it, neither do you). While we may have missed-out on their good/bad perceptions of the brand, we were still able to organically capture cosmetics category insights by the way the questions were crafted.

- The companies we work with approve the projects before they are distributed, so sensitive information is never leaked.

While, confidentiality might seem like a deal-breaker at first, give it a bit of thought and you'll find that measures can always be taken to keep things under wraps.

8. **Don't use evaluation approaches for exploration needs:** When Henry Ford was out <u>exploring</u> new ideas, he avoided only asking his customers for their thoughts,

because he knew many of them would have recommend a "faster horse." Of course, when the time came to <u>evaluate</u> his new "automobile" concept, he probably went to his customers for their feedback and they must have said, *"Wow! That's a great idea! We never would have thought of that. We would have told you to create a faster horse."*

The problem is, brands and companies have been so brainwashed by the silly notion that *"the target audience and core customer know all,"* they often only enlist these sources to both explore <u>and</u> evaluate ideas. Remind yourself that these are two completely separate objectives that require different sources. When you are exploring for new ideas, go beyond your target audience and your core customers to get all different perspectives. Once you've created the ideas, then go and enlist your target audience and core customers to help you evaluate them.

9. **Don't get sucked into the "I have to use a collaboration platform" trap:** There are lots of collaboration platforms that you can use to support your open-source efforts and some of them are pretty sexy. However, you need to always remind yourself that open-source collaboration is NOT about the platform you use, it's about the PEOPLE you collaborate with. Visionary, Seth Godin, put it best in his book *Tribes* when he wrote:

Please Note! Throughout this book, I'm pretty quick to use examples based on the Internet and some of the astonishing new tools that are showing up to enable tribes to be more effective. But the Internet is just a tool, an easy way to enable some tactics. The real power of tribes has nothing to do with the Internet and everything to do with <u>people</u>.

Don't get caught up in all the hype surrounding those collaboration platforms. The approach you use to collaborate should be the one that works best for your members and your organization. So, consider everything – from online survey platforms to face-to-face meetings to good ol' email.

10. **Incorporate incentives and rewards:** Whenever I discuss my company someone always asks, *"How do you incentivize your BigHeads?"* I'm not going to discuss our incentive structure, because that's part of the reward of being a member of our group, but I will say that we've developed an approach that works for us.

Having an incentive structure in place is absolutely necessary if you want to keep your collaborators involved and interested. It's up to you to figure out what will best motivate them and you should consider lots of approaches – from cash prizes to gifts to a piece of the action.

11. **Apply it anywhere:** Even though this book is called *Brand Opening* and features many brand-centric examples, remember that the core methodology can be applied to other teams in your organization and even beyond the business world to everyday situations. Just ask the hospital that ended up learning from the pit crew.

12. **Don't make excuses:** If you made it this far, you might be interested in giving open-source collaboration a shot. However, I can tell you that when the time comes for you to pull-the-trigger, many of you won't do it.

I can't even begin to count the number of times I introduce

the approach to companies that are gung-ho to give it a shot, but end up never doing it. Of course, they always have a list of reasons and excuses, just like many of you will. You might tell yourself that you don't have the budget. You might tell yourself that your senior management would never go for something like this. You might tell yourself that your existing innovation process is good enough. And the list goes on…and on…and on.

I'll admit, trying something new can be uncomfortable, scary and seem risky. But if your job is to generate new thinking, it's going to be a lot riskier to continue doing what you've always done. At some point, your competition or someone else in your organization is going to bring a new approach to the table that will generate bigger and better ideas and you're going to be left in the dust. I guess that cheesy, *"not taking a risk is the biggest risk"* cliché is actually true after all!

13. **Ask yourself a simple question:** If you're still wondering if this approach is right for you, just ask yourself the following question and watch how quickly it puts everything in perspective:

If you already have creative minds and experts from <u>WITHIN</u> your industry thinking about your brand or objective, why wouldn't you *have creative minds and experts from <u>OUTSIDE</u> your industry thinking about your brand or objective too?*

Now, go OPEN YOUR BRAND!

Good luck!

104

Notes

p. 10-11. "Open Source started when programmers began collaborating online to build new technical platforms and systems. Freed from institutional red-tape, hierarchy and shareholder responsibility the ideas flowed fast and furious through these online communities. At the heart of the process was the community's willingness to share programming 'source code', albeit under certain conditions. And so the Open Source Movement was born. By any measure, the results have been staggering. Linux, a computer operating system, was one of the first big breakthroughs" This quote is from James Cherkoff's manifesto, *"What is Open Source Marketing?"* (2005).

p. 11-12. "The Creative Commons license is a new type of copyright (nicknamed copyleft) created by an Open Source community that gives artists the flexibility to collaborate. Wikipedia is an Open Source encyclopedia containing 1.3 million articles in eight different languages, all written, developed and maintained by people around the world. Ohmynews is an Open

Source Korean newspaper written by more than 40,000 individual citizens." This quote is from James Cherkoff's manifesto, *"What is Open Source Marketing?"* (2005).

p. 17. "According to Brannon, marketing can get 'tired and a bit vanilla' when those involved are too close to the brand. He added: 'I believe that the ideas that you get from people who are not that close to your brand are often a little bit richer.'" This excerpt was taken from the *Marketing Magazine.co.uk* article *"Chevrolet Set for TV Return With Crowd-sourced Ad."* By Gemma Charles. (July 6, 2010).

p. 19. "For Mr. Parker and other CEOs, the must- see list is growing in number and variety. Nike has long used team sponsorships and star athlete endorsements to market its products and sought advice from athletes for its designs. But he also spends time with musicians, graffiti artists and other creative talent. 'I meet regularly with our biggest retail customers but I also go off the beaten path where I can stimulate the right side of my brain -- and discover new tastes in music, fashion, cuisine,' he says." This excerpt was taken from *The Wall*

Street Journal article, *"CEOs Are Spending More Quality Time With Their Customers."* By Carol Hymowitz. (May 14, 2007).

p. 25. "Innovation by users, provides a very necessary complement to and feedback for manufacturer innovation." This quote was taken from Eric Von Hippel's book, *Democratizing Innovation.* (2005).

p. 29-30. "The place where different disciplines, cultures and backgrounds connect to form new ideas and solutions for long-standing problems." This quote was taken from Frans Johansson's book, *The Medici Effect: Breakthrough Insights at the Intersection of Ideas, Concepts, and Cultures.* (2004).

p. 30-32. This is a summary of *The Wall Street Journal* article, *"Hospital Races to Learn Lessons of Ferrari Pit Crew."* By Gautam Naik, (November 14, 2006).

p. 91. "P&G's development and implementation of 'Connect and Develop' has unfolded over many years. There have been some hiccups along the way, but largely it has been a methodical process of learning by doing, abandoning what doesn't work and expanding what does." This quote was taken from the *Harvard Business Review* article, *"Connect and Develop: Inside Procter & Gamble's New Model for Innovation."* By Larry Huston and Nabil Sakkab. (Mar 01, 2006).

p. 97. "Please Note! Throughout this book, I'm pretty quick to use examples based on the Internet and some of the astonishing new tools that are showing up to enable tribes to be more effective. But the Internet is just a tool, an easy way to enable some tactics. The real power of tribes has nothing to do with the Internet and everything to do with people." This quote was taken from Seth Godin's book, *Tribes. We need You To Lead Us.* (2008).

About the Author

For more than 20 years John Palumbo has been developing unique and innovative ideas, insights, campaigns and solutions for brands and companies. In fact, he is credited with inventing the iconic "pop-up store" approach after launching the Nintendo Game Cube in 2001. His opinions, work and approaches have been featured in *Fast Company*, *Forbes*, *Business 2.0*, *Investor's Business Daily*, *The New York Times*, *The Wall Street Journal*, *Advertising Age*, *Brandweek* and a host of other national/local/trade outlets. He has also been published by numerous marketing trade publications and he regularly speaks at companies and industry conferences about innovation and open-source collaboration.

In 2006, John founded BigHeads Network, which is one of the first companies to formally bring open-source collaboration principles to brands and companies via a turnkey solution.